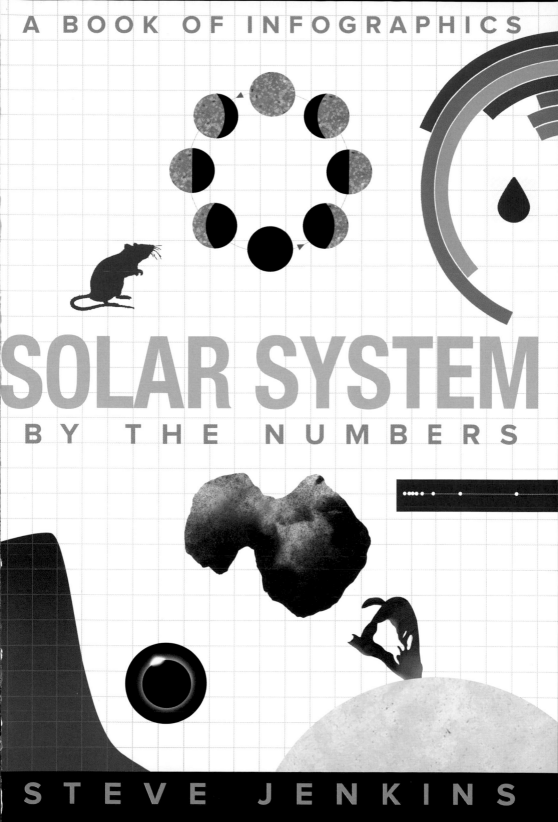

A BOOK OF INFOGRAPHICS

SOLAR SYSTEM

BY THE NUMBERS

STEVE JENKINS

HOUGHTON MIFFLIN HARCOURT · BOSTON · NEW YORK

Contents

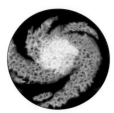

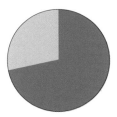
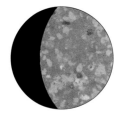

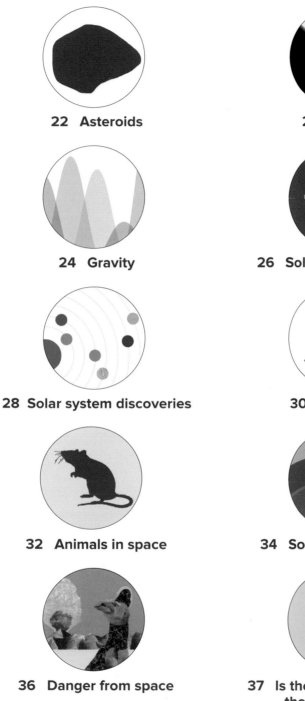

The Milky Way Galaxy

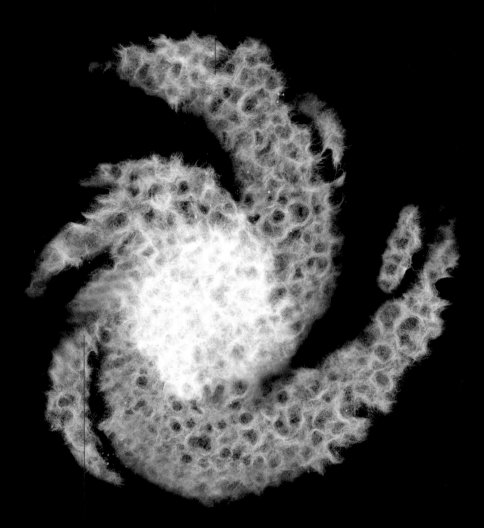

The solar system is here
(but it would be too small to
see in this image).

We live on a small, rocky planet. That planet circles a small, yellow sun. That sun is found near the outer edge of the Milky Way Galaxy. Galaxies are collections of stars—lots of stars. There are hundreds of billions of stars in our galaxy alone. And there are hundreds of billions of other galaxies.

In this book, we'll stay closer to home. We'll use infographics—charts, graphs, and diagrams—to take a closer look at our own Sun and the planets, moons, and other objects that circle it. This is our solar system.

* Words in blue can be found in the glossary on page 38.

What's in our solar system?

Next to some of the giant stars in our galaxy, the Sun is not very big. But compared to everything else in the solar system, it is huge. It contains almost all the matter in the solar system.

Sun

All the matter in the solar system

The thin red slice of the circle represents all the matter in the solar system that is *not* part of the Sun.

Eight planets
The planets orbit the Sun.

Six named dwarf planets, including Pluto
Several more dwarf planets will soon be added to the list. And there may be thousands more dwarf planets not yet discovered.

More than 350 moons
Moons are bodies that orbit the planets, dwarf planets, or asteroids.

Hundreds of thousands of asteroids
The current asteroid count is more than 780,000.

Thousands of comets
There are probably as many as a trillion more comets in orbits far from the Sun.

Uncountable numbers of rocks and dust particles

Our star

The word "solar" means "of the Sun."

Temperature at the center of the Sun

27 million⁰F (15 million⁰C)

Temperature of the Sun's surface

10,000⁰F (5,538⁰C)

Temperature of sunspots (cooler areas on the Sun's surface)

6,400⁰F (3,500⁰C)

Earth (shown here at the same scale as the Sun)

Huge jets of hot gas flare from the Sun. They can be many times larger than Earth.

A note about temperatures:
F (Fahrenheit) and C (Celsius) are two different temperature scales.

The Sun's life cycle

4¹/₂ billion years ago

A huge cloud of dust and gas collapses and gets hotter and hotter. The Sun is born.

From about 4 billion years ago to 4 billion years from now

The Sun is a yellow dwarf star, a common type of star in our galaxy.

5 billion years from now

The Sun expands and becomes a red giant star. Earth may be swallowed up by the Sun. But long before that happens, our planet is burned to a crisp.

8 billion years from now

The Sun becomes a white dwarf star, not much larger than Earth but much heavier.

What is an eclipse?

When the Moon passes directly between Earth and the Sun, the Moon casts a shadow on Earth's surface. It's a solar eclipse! When Earth casts its shadow on the Moon, it's called a lunar eclipse.

From Earth, the Sun and Moon appear to be the same size. The Sun is really much larger than the Moon, but it is much farther away.

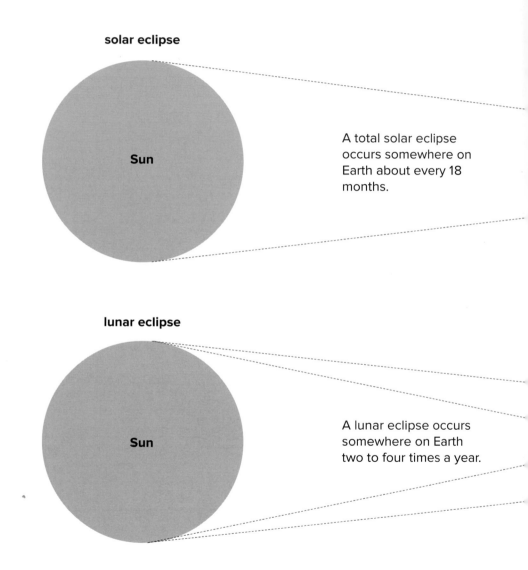

solar eclipse

Sun

A total solar eclipse occurs somewhere on Earth about every 18 months.

lunar eclipse

Sun

A lunar eclipse occurs somewhere on Earth two to four times a year.

Note: Sizes and distances in these diagrams are not to scale.

During a total solar eclipse, the glowing atmosphere of the Sun shows around the edges of the Moon.

The shadow of a solar eclipse travels in a 70-mile-wide (110-kilometer-wide) path.

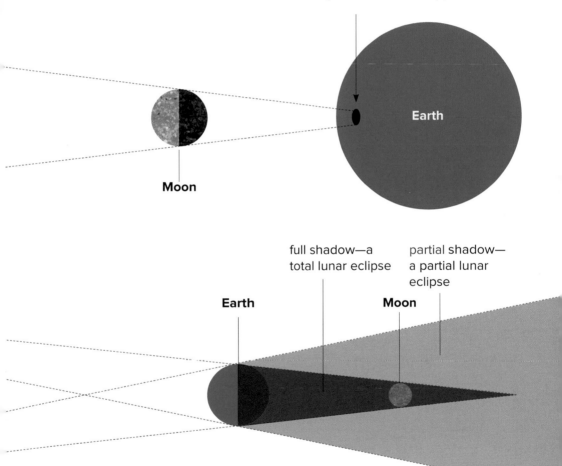

Earth

Moon

full shadow—a total lunar eclipse

partial shadow— a partial lunar eclipse

Earth

Moon

During a total lunar eclipse, light passing through Earth's atmosphere makes the Moon appear red (for the same reason a sunset often looks reddish).

Circling the Sun

All the objects in the solar system—planets, moons, asteroids, and comets—travel in an orbit around the Sun.

This diagram shows the relative distances of the planets from the Sun, but not their actual size. The planets would be too small to see at this scale.

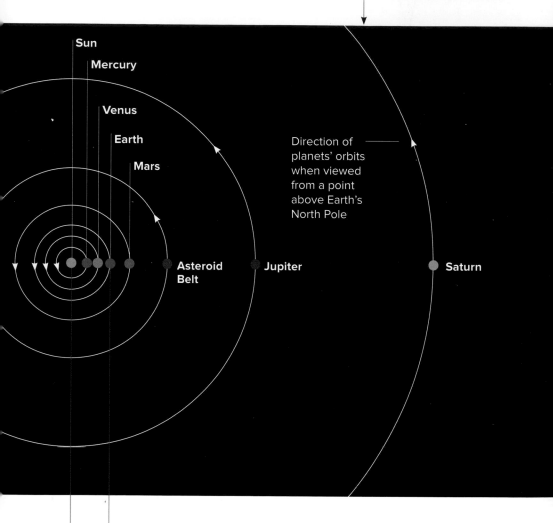

Sun

Mercury

Venus

Earth

Mars

Direction of planets' orbits when viewed from a point above Earth's North Pole

Asteroid Belt

Jupiter

Saturn

1 AU

Measuring the solar system

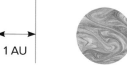

An **AU**, or **astronomical unit**, is the distance between Earth and the Sun (not shown at actual scale). Astronomers often use AUs to measure distances in the solar system.

If the **Sun** were the size of a tennis ball . . .

. . . **Earth** would be this big. It would be almost 23 feet (7 meters) away.

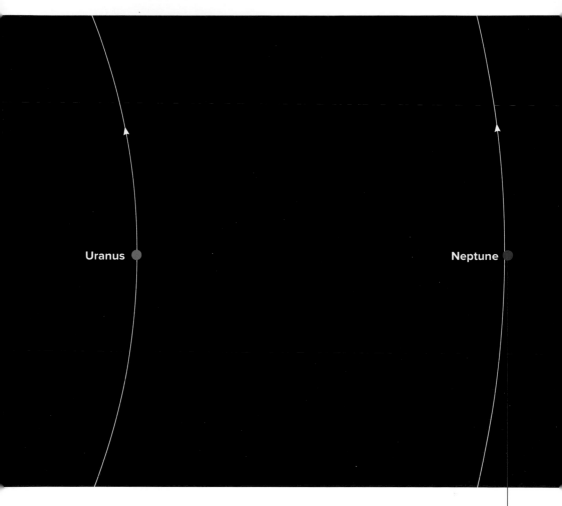

Uranus

Neptune

Neptune is 30 AUs from the Sun.

It is 93 million miles (150 million kilometers) from Earth to the Sun. This is one AU.

How big are the planets?

The inner, or rocky, planets

The gas giants

Venus Mars

Moon

Mercury | Earth

Jupiter

Sun

One million Earths could fit inside the Sun. And 1,300 Earths could fit inside Jupiter.

The Sun is as wide as 109 Earths.

The Sun and the planets are shown here at the same scale.

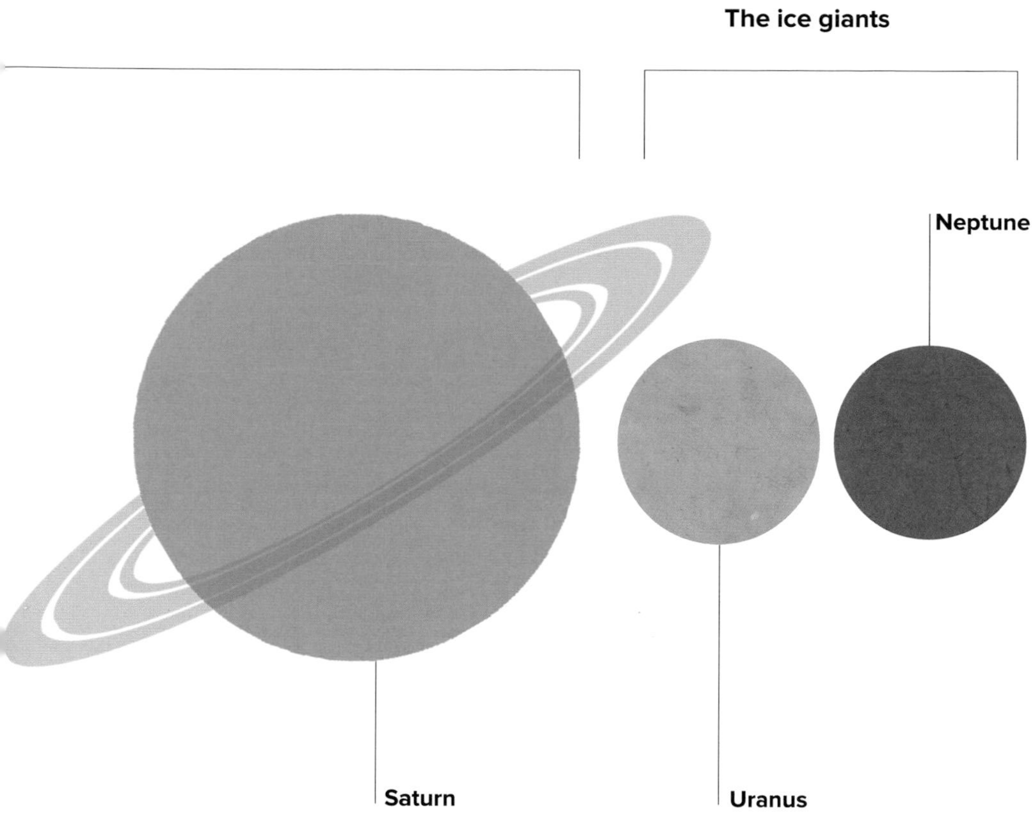

The ice giants

Neptune

Saturn

Uranus

● **Pluto**
(a dwarf planet)

When Pluto was discovered in 1930, it became the solar system's ninth planet. But in 2006, astronomers decided that Pluto is actually a dwarf planet. This left the solar system with just eight planets.

The inner planets

The four planets closest to the Sun are known as the inner, or rocky, planets. They are shown here at the same scale.

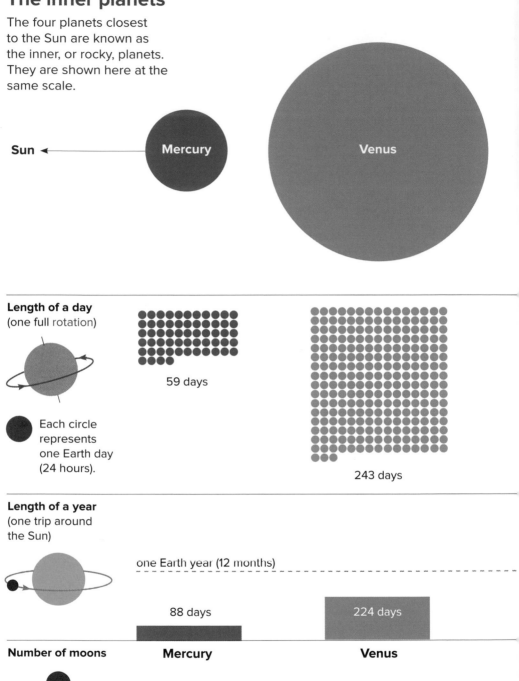

Sun ◄——————— Mercury

Venus

Length of a day
(one full rotation)

59 days

Each circle represents one Earth day (24 hours).

243 days

Length of a year
(one trip around the Sun)

one Earth year (12 months)

88 days

224 days

Number of moons

Mercury

Venus

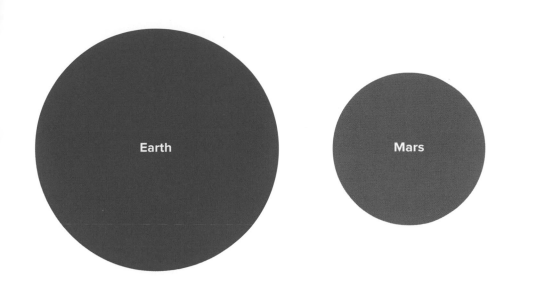

Earth

Mars

24 hours

24 hours, 37 minutes

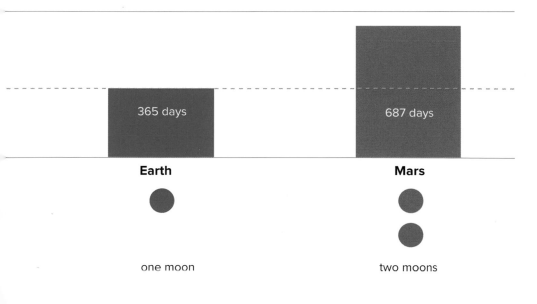

365 days

687 days

Earth

Mars

one moon

two moons

The outer planets

The four outer planets are mostly made of gas and ice. They are shown here at the same scale.

The gas giants

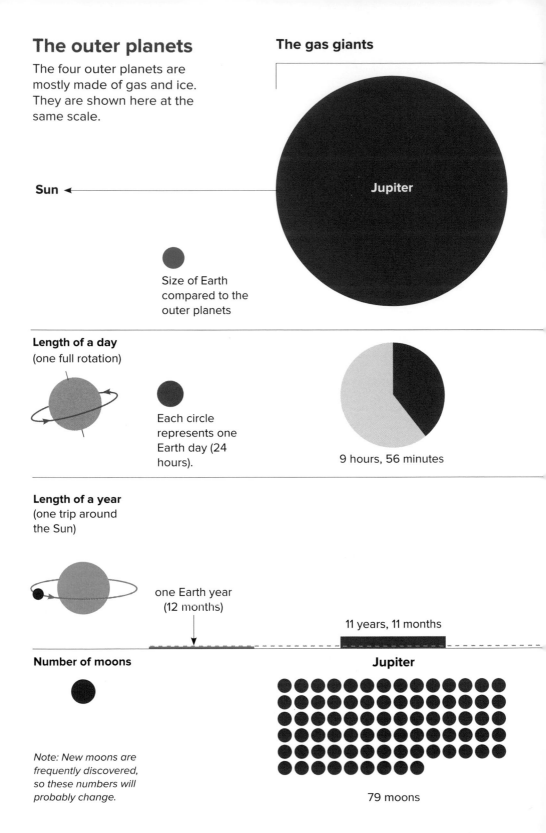

Sun ←

Jupiter

Size of Earth compared to the outer planets

Length of a day
(one full rotation)

Each circle represents one Earth day (24 hours).

9 hours, 56 minutes

Length of a year
(one trip around the Sun)

one Earth year (12 months)

11 years, 11 months

Number of moons

Note: New moons are frequently discovered, so these numbers will probably change.

Jupiter

79 moons

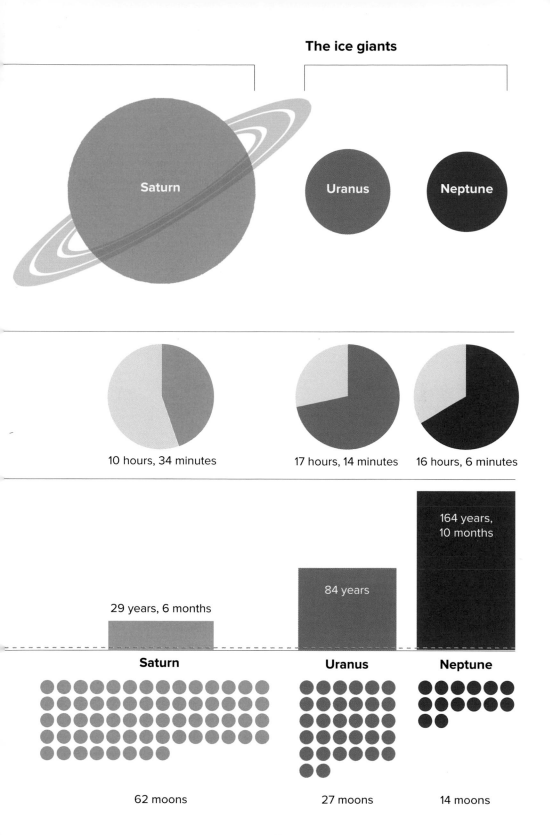

The ice giants

Saturn

Uranus

Neptune

10 hours, 34 minutes

17 hours, 14 minutes

16 hours, 6 minutes

164 years,
10 months

84 years

29 years, 6 months

Saturn

Uranus

Neptune

62 moons

27 moons

14 moons

Earth's Moon

Our Moon is the brightest object in the night sky. It's the only place in the solar system—besides Earth—that humans have visited.

The Moon is slowly moving away from Earth. It gets this much farther away each year.

The phases of the Moon

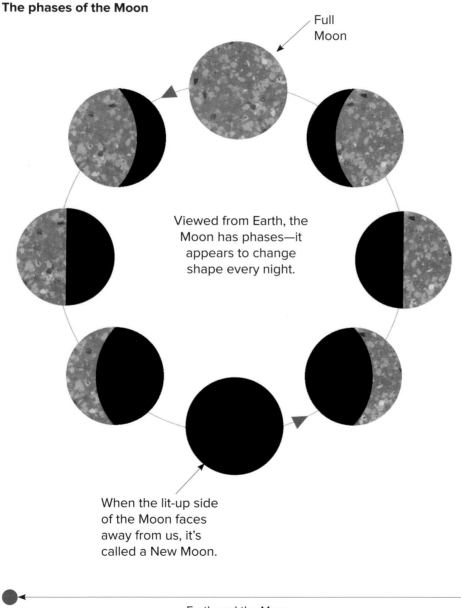

Full Moon

Viewed from Earth, the Moon has phases—it appears to change shape every night.

When the lit-up side of the Moon faces away from us, it's called a New Moon.

Earth and the Moon, showing size and distance at the same scale

Other solar system moons

A moon is a body that orbits a planet, dwarf planet, or asteroid. There are more than 200 moons in our solar system. If a moon is large enough for its own gravity to pull it into a round shape, it is called a *major moon*.

Deimos, a moon of Mars, is small and oddly shaped.

The gravity of a major moon is strong enough to pull it into a sphere.

Major moons of the solar system

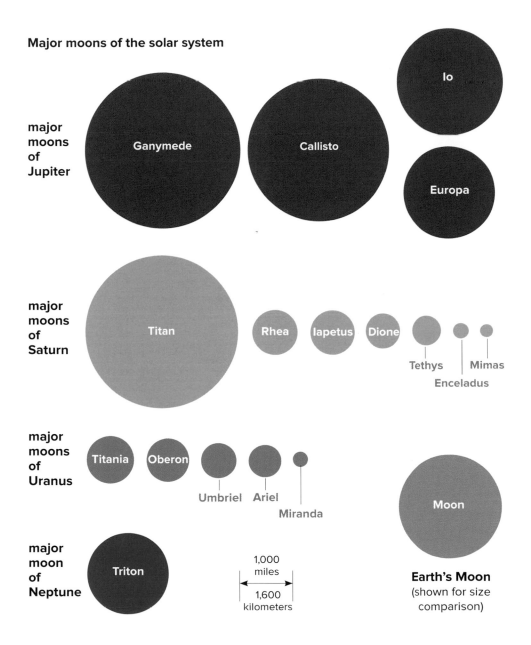

major moons of Jupiter

Ganymede
Callisto
Io
Europa

major moons of Saturn

Titan
Rhea
Iapetus
Dione
Tethys
Enceladus
Mimas

major moons of Uranus

Titania
Oberon
Umbriel
Ariel
Miranda

major moon of Neptune

Triton

1,000 miles
1,600 kilometers

Moon

Earth's Moon
(shown for size comparison)

Asteroids

Between the orbits of Mars and Jupiter are hundreds of millions of asteroids—chunks of rock and ice. They range in size from a few feet across to hundreds of miles in diameter. This part of the solar system is known as the asteroid belt.

Note: This diagram is not to scale.

Mars

Jupiter

Asteroid Belt

Ida

35 miles (54 kilometers)

Dactyl

This tiny moon is about one mile (1½ kilometers) across.

The asteroid **Ida** looks like a baked potato. And it has a moon of its own, called **Dactyl**. This is the first moon of an asteroid that has been discovered.

Sometimes a piece of an asteroid—or a fragment of a comet—enters Earth's atmosphere. It is called a meteor, or shooting star. If the space rock hits the ground, it is called a meteorite.

Comets

Comets are found in the outer reaches of the solar system, far from the Sun. They are balls of rock, dirt, and ice up to sixty miles (97 kilometers) across.

We have identified a few thousand comets, but there are probably billions or trillions of comets orbiting the Sun.

When a comet approaches the Sun, a tail of melted ice and dust streams out behind it. This tail always points away from the Sun.

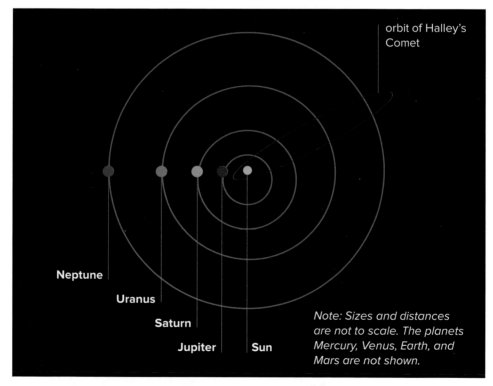

orbit of Halley's Comet

Neptune

Uranus

Saturn

Jupiter

Sun

Note: Sizes and distances are not to scale. The planets Mercury, Venus, Earth, and Mars are not shown.

The most famous comet is **Halley's Comet**. It makes an orbit about every 76 years, and it can easily be seen without a telescope. Halley's Comet will return in 2061.

Many comets make regular orbits of the Sun, some every few years. Other comets take as long as 30 million years to complete one orbit.

Gravity

How high could a person jump on another moon or planet if they can jump three feet high on Earth?

18 feet
(5½ meters)

5 feet
(1½ meters)

4 feet
(122 centimeters)

3 feet
(91 centimeters)

2 feet
(61 centimeters)

1 foot
(30 centimeters)

Gravity is weaker on a small planet. The less gravity there is, the higher a person could jump.

Mercury   **Venus**   **Earth**   **Moon**

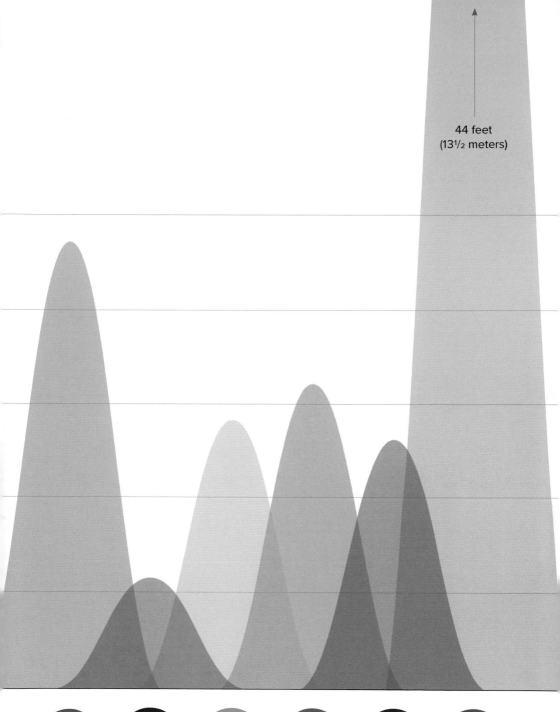

44 feet
(13½ meters)

Mars   Jupiter   Saturn   Uranus   Neptune   Pluto

Solar system weather

Rain and snow

Earth isn't the only place in the solar system where it rains or snows. But precipitation in other places can be unusual.

 On **Venus** it rains sulfuric acid.

 On **Titan**, a moon of Saturn, it rains methane (liquid natural gas).

It may rain diamonds on **Jupiter** and other gas giant and ice giant planets.

 Carbon dioxide falls as snow on the poles of **Mars**.

 On **Enceladus**, a moon of Saturn, frozen water falls as snow.

Average temperatures

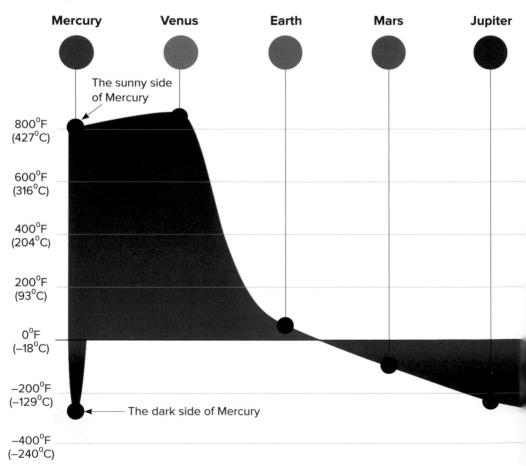

Mercury   Venus   Earth   Mars   Jupiter

The sunny side of Mercury

800°F (427°C)

600°F (316°C)

400°F (204°C)

200°F (93°C)

0°F (−18°C)

−200°F (−129°C) — The dark side of Mercury

−400°F (−240°C)

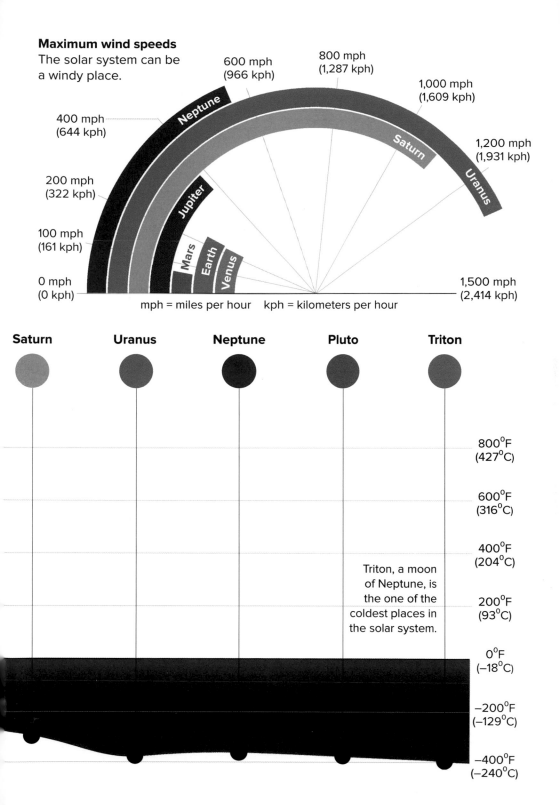

Maximum wind speeds
The solar system can be a windy place.

600 mph (966 kph)

800 mph (1,287 kph)

1,000 mph (1,609 kph)

400 mph (644 kph)

Neptune

1,200 mph (1,931 kph)

Saturn

Uranus

200 mph (322 kph)

Jupiter

100 mph (161 kph)

Mars

Earth

Venus

0 mph (0 kph)

1,500 mph (2,414 kph)

mph = miles per hour   kph = kilometers per hour

Saturn   Uranus   Neptune   Pluto   Triton

800°F (427°C)

600°F (316°C)

400°F (204°C)

Triton, a moon of Neptune, is the one of the coldest places in the solar system.

200°F (93°C)

0°F (−18°C)

−200°F (−129°C)

−400°F (−240°C)

Solar system discoveries

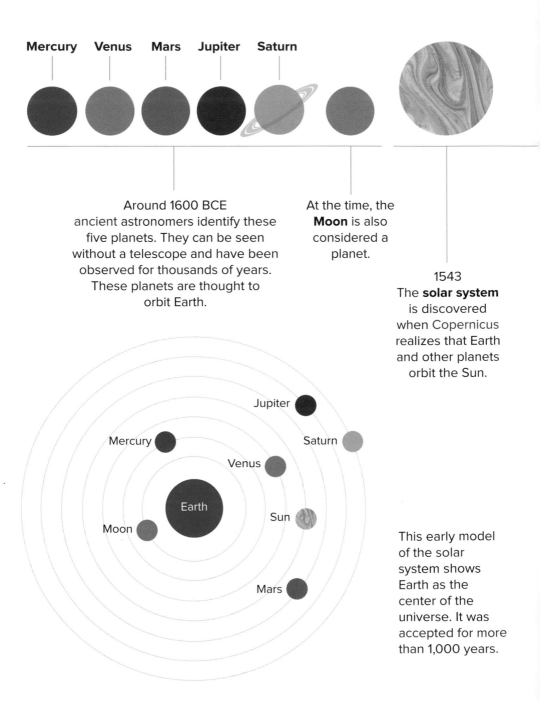

Mercury   Venus   Mars   Jupiter   Saturn

Around 1600 BCE ancient astronomers identify these five planets. They can be seen without a telescope and have been observed for thousands of years. These planets are thought to orbit Earth.

At the time, the **Moon** is also considered a planet.

1543
The **solar system** is discovered when Copernicus realizes that Earth and other planets orbit the Sun.

Jupiter

Mercury

Saturn

Venus

Earth

Sun

Moon

Mars

This early model of the solar system shows Earth as the center of the universe. It was accepted for more than 1,000 years.

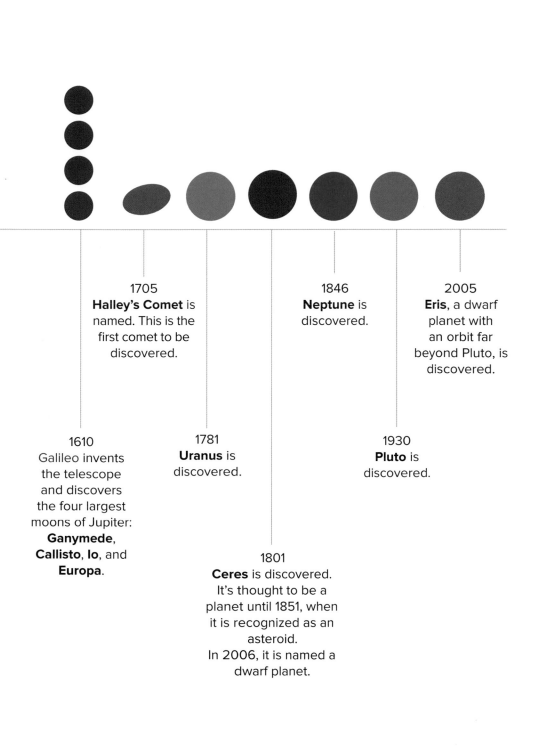

1705
Halley's Comet is named. This is the first comet to be discovered.

1846
Neptune is discovered.

2005
Eris, a dwarf planet with an orbit far beyond Pluto, is discovered.

1610
Galileo invents the telescope and discovers the four largest moons of Jupiter: **Ganymede, Callisto, Io**, and **Europa**.

1781
Uranus is discovered.

1930
Pluto is discovered.

1801
Ceres is discovered. It's thought to be a planet until 1851, when it is recognized as an asteroid.
In 2006, it is named a dwarf planet.

Exploration

How many times have we visited other places in the solar system?*

Sun	
Sun	🛰🛰🛰🛰🛰🛰🛰🛰
Mercury	🛰🛰🛰🛰 🚀
Venus	🛰🛰🛰🛰🛰🛰🛰🛰 🚀🚀🚀🚀🚀🚀🚀🚀
Mars	🛰🛰🛰🛰🛰🛰🛰🛰 🚀🚀🚀🚀🚀🚀🚀
Asteroids	🛰🛰🛰🛰🛰🛰🛰🛰 🚀🚀🚀🚀
Jupiter	🛰🛰🛰🛰🛰🛰🛰🛰 🚀
Saturn	🛰🛰🛰🛰
Uranus	🛰
Neptune	🛰
Pluto (dwarf planet)	🛰

*As of the end of 2018.

New missions take place frequently, so these numbers will change.

Some of the visits in the chart were made by spacecraft that traveled to more than one planet or moon.

Orbited or flew by   Landed or crashed on the surface   Visits to comets and other planet's moons are not shown.

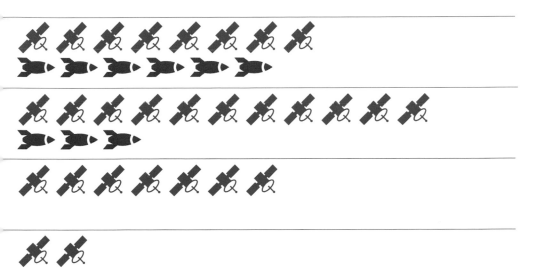

We have explored Earth's Moon more than any other place in the solar system

 37 orbiters   30 unmanned landers   Six human missions have landed on the Moon. Twelve astronauts have walked on its surface.

Animals in space

Humans aren't the only earthlings that have traveled off the planet. From the earliest days of space exploration, animals have been launched into space.

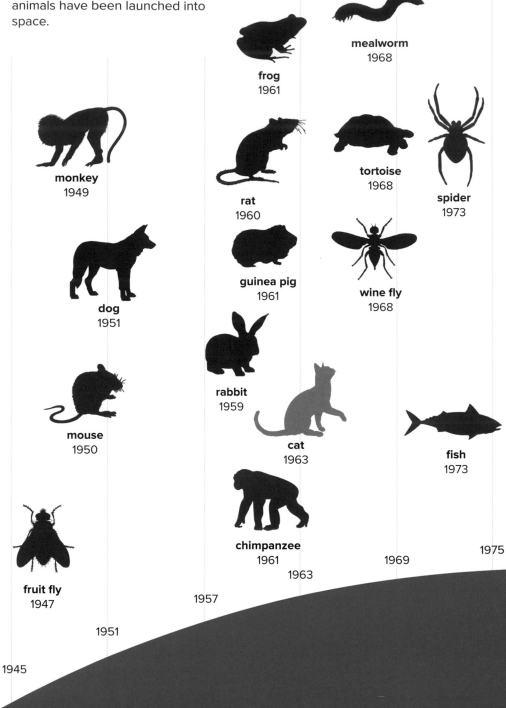

mealworm
1968

frog
1961

monkey
1949

rat
1960

tortoise
1968

spider
1973

dog
1951

guinea pig
1961

wine fly
1968

rabbit
1959

mouse
1950

cat
1963

fish
1973

fruit fly
1947

chimpanzee
1961

1963

1969

1975

1957

1951

1945

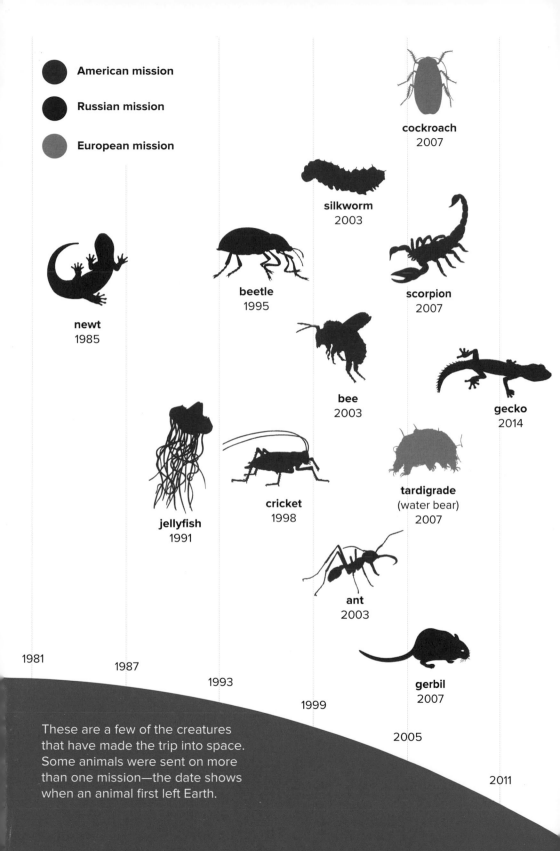

American mission

Russian mission

European mission

cockroach
2007

silkworm
2003

beetle
1995

scorpion
2007

newt
1985

bee
2003

gecko
2014

jellyfish
1991

cricket
1998

tardigrade
(water bear)
2007

ant
2003

1981

1987

1993

1999

gerbil
2007

These are a few of the creatures
that have made the trip into space.
Some animals were sent on more
than one mission—the date shows
when an animal first left Earth.

2005

2011

Solar system oceans

Scientists believe there are at least nine solar system planets, dwarf planets, or moons with liquid water oceans. These are the most likely places for life to exist in the solar system.

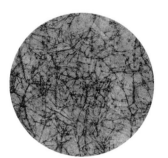

The oceans of the solar system moons are covered by a thick layer of ice. The surface of Jupiter's moon **Europa**, above, is marked by cracks in the ice.

Amount of water on solar system planets, dwarf planets, and moons

27X as much water as on Earth

4X as much water as on Earth

2X as much water as on Earth

Earth	Europa	Callisto	Ganymede

moons of Jupiter

The size of solar system moons and dwarf planets with oceans (compared to Earth)

Some of these oceans contain much
more water than the seas on Earth.

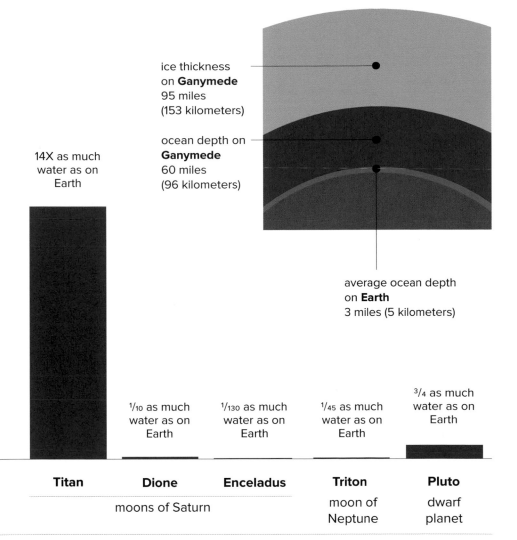

ice thickness
on **Ganymede**
95 miles
(153 kilometers)

ocean depth on
Ganymede
60 miles
(96 kilometers)

14X as much
water as on
Earth

average ocean depth
on **Earth**
3 miles (5 kilometers)

$^1/_{10}$ as much
water as on
Earth

$^1/_{130}$ as much
water as on
Earth

$^1/_{45}$ as much
water as on
Earth

$^3/_4$ as much
water as on
Earth

Titan   **Dione**   **Enceladus**   **Triton**   **Pluto**

moons of Saturn   moon of   dwarf
                         Neptune   planet

Danger from space

Sometimes an asteroid or comet crashes into Earth. Even a small asteroid can cause serious damage. A large one can threaten most life on our planet. Fortunately, these collisions are rare.

Impacts	How big is the object?	About how often does one hit Earth?	What are the effects of the impact?*
	150 feet (46 meters)	1,000 years	destroys a small city
	330 feet (100 meters)	5,000 years	destroys a large city
	1/2 mile (800 meters)	250,000 years	destroys a small country; some worldwide climate effects
	6 miles (10 kilometers)	100 million years	global destruction, mass extinctions of plants and animals

An asteroid six miles (10 kilometers) across crashed into Earth 66 million years ago. It was probably responsible for killing off the dinosaurs.

The effects of an impact vary with the speed, angle of entry, and composition of an asteroid or comet.

Is there life elsewhere in the solar system?

So far, Earth is only place we know of where life exists. But there are other places in the solar system that could support life. Here are a few of the most interesting.

Life as we know it needs liquid water to exist. Water can probably be found on several moons and at least one other planet.

Mars

Some scientists think this is the most likely place to find life beyond Earth.

Liquid water beneath the surface could be home to microscopic organisms.

Enceladus
(moon of Saturn)

Ganymede
Callisto
Europa
(moons of Jupiter)

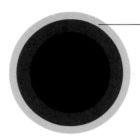

These moons have liquid oceans beneath a thick layer of ice. It's possible life could exist in these waters.

Two places where strange forms of life might exist without water:

Venus

The surface is too hot for life. But high above the surface, drifting microbes might feed on chemicals in the clouds.

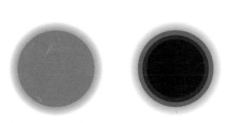

Titan

This moon of Saturn has rain, rivers, and lakes. But the liquid isn't water—it's similar to the gas we put into our cars.

What would life on other moons or planets look like?

We haven't found it, so we don't know. But there is a good chance that if life exists, it will in the form of small, simple organisms.

Perhaps life elsewhere will be similar to bacteria on Earth.

It almost certainly won't look like the aliens in movies and TV shows.

Glossary

ancient
A time long ago; in the distant past.

astronomer
A scientist who studies space and the objects in it, including planets, moons, stars, and comets.

atmosphere
The gases—held in place by gravity— around a star, planet, or moon.

bacteria
Tiny, one-celled organisms. They are too small to see without magnification.

carbon dioxide
A colorless gas that exists naturally in Earth's atmosphere. It is used by plants to make food and exhaled in the breath of animals.

Copernicus
A Polish astronomer who lived about 500 years ago. He realized that rather than being at the center of the universe, Earth orbits the Sun.

diameter
The distance across something; twice the radius.

diamonds
The element carbon in the form of a crystal. Diamonds are one of the hardest substances we know of. They are used as gemstones and can be extremely valuable.

dwarf planet
An object that orbits the Sun. It is large enough for its own gravity to pull it into a round shape, but it is not a planet.

flare
A sudden burst of brightness on the Sun's surface.

Galileo
An Italian astronomer and scientist who lived about 400 years ago. He built one of the first telescopes and used it to observe the solar system.

gas
Matter that has no fixed shape or volume. A gas will fill whatever container holds it.

gravity
The force that attracts matter to other matter. It holds moons and planets together and keeps them in an orbit around the Sun.

infographics
Facts and information presented visually as diagrams, charts, and graphs rather than just text.

lunar
Relating to the Moon.

mass extinctions
Events that caused more than half of Earth's living species to die out.

matter
A substance that has mass and takes up space.

methane
A colorless, flammable gas that is produced by the breakdown of vegetation. Methane is the main component of the natural gas we often use to heat our homes.

microbes, or microscopic organisms
Forms of life that are too small to see without magnification, including bacteria, viruses, and fungi.

Milky Way Galaxy
The galaxy that contains our Sun and hundreds of billions of other stars.

orbit
The path of one body in space around another, such as Earth's path around the Sun.

organism
An individual living thing.

partial
Part of something; not complete.

particles
Tiny pieces of matter.

precipitation
Rain, sleet, or snow. It can be composed of water or other chemicals.

red giant
A giant star with a cooler surface that glows red. It is one of the last stages of a star's life.

rotation
Spinning or rotating around an axis.

sulfuric acid
A liquid chemical compound that can dissolve skin, metals, and many other substances.

white dwarf
A very dense star that has used up most of its fuel and collapsed. When the Sun becomes a white dwarf, it will be about the size of Earth.

yellow dwarf
A star similar in size to the Sun that glows white or yellow. Our Sun is a yellow dwarf.

Bibliography

The Cambridge Photographic Guide to the Planets. By F. W. Taylor. Cambridge University Press, 2001.

Cosmos: The Infographic Book of Space. By Stuart Lowe and Chris North. Aurum Press, 2015.

DK Find Out! Solar System. DK Publishing, 2016.

Empire of the Sun. By John Gribben and Simon Goodwin. New York University Press, 1998.

Otherworlds: Visions of Our Solar System. By Michael Benson. Abrams, 2017.

Our Solar System. By Seymour Simon. Harper, 2014.

The Planets: The Definitive Visual Guide to Our Solar System. By Robert Dinwiddie. DK Publishing, 2014.

Solar System. By Marcus Chown. Black Dog & Leventhal, 2011.

Space Encyclopedia: A Tour of Our Solar System and Beyond. By David A. Aguilar. National Geographic Children's Books, 2013.

For Alvin

All rights reserved. For information about permission to reproduce
selections from this book, write to trade.permissions@hmhco.com
or to Permissions, Houghton Mifflin Harcourt Publishing Company,
3 Park Avenue, 19th Floor, New York, New York 10016.

hmhbooks.com

The illustrations are cut- and torn-paper collage.
The infographics are cut-paper silhouettes and graphics created digitally.
The text type was set in Proxima Nova.
The display type was set in Berthold Akzidenz Grotesk.

ISBN: 978-1-328-85097-3 hardcover
ISBN: 978-1-328-85098-0 paperback

Manufactured in China
SCP 10 9 8 7 6 5 4 3 2 1
4500794430